A Clash of Cultures

A Clash of Cultures

Fort Bowie and the Chiricahua Apaches

by Robert M. Utley

Division of Publications

National Park Service

Washington, D.C.

1977

About the Author

ROBERT M. UTLEY is currently deputy
executive director of the Advisory Council
on Historic Preservation. He is a specialist
in western American history and was one of
the founders of the Western History
Association. He has written many articles
and several books on Indians and the Army.
He also serves on the board of advisers of
the National Historical Society and the
Center for American Indian History at the
Newberry Library in Chicago.

Contents

This is a detail of a map drawn in 1864 so it does not show all the places mentioned in the text. Note that Fort McDowell is incorrectly located on the original, and also that the Fort Grant on the original was an active post from 1860 to 1872. The Fort Grant shown in black was active from 1872-1907.

ARIZONA NEW MEXICO

• Fort Verde

• Fort McDowell

• Fort Apache

• Gila River

San Carlos
Reservation

• Fort Breckinridge

• Fort Thomas

• Fort Grant

• Bowie Station

• Fort Lowell

• Fort Bowie

• Camp John A. Rucker

Fort Crittenden

• Fort Huachuca

Fort Buchanan

• Cañon de los Embudos

Scale

On September 8, 1886, soldiers and Indians gathered on the parade ground of a frontier post nestled amid cactus-studded hills. A cordon of blueclad troopers formed around a train of open wagons loaded with Indian families. As a military band drawn up at the base of the flagstaff played "Auld Lang Syne," the procession moved out of the fort and headed north.

The post was Fort Bowie, Arizona, for a quarter of a century a lonely bastion in Apache Pass, the heart of Apacheria. The Indians were Geronimo and his band of Chiricahua Apaches, for more than a decade scourges of the southwestern frontier. Now the warfare had ended, and with a touch of musical irony the victors bade farewell as the vanquished were escorted to the railroad cars that would bear them eastward to an uncertain future.

Today the gaunt ruins of Fort Bowie, set in an environment otherwise uncluttered by man's works, recall a dramatic and significant phase of the American past—the struggle of a dynamic and aggressive people to conquer the wilderness, and the struggle of a proud and independent people to retain the wilderness and the way of life they had known.

Two young men wearing typical Apache garb have their picture taken at the San Carlos Agency in late 1888.

The Land and the People

The Apaches originally lived in the Great Plains, but in the 16th century they began to drift westward. Two hundred years later they had spread into the desert-and-mountain country we know as the American Southwest and had claimed Apache Pass as their own—a long time before white men gave it the name it bears today. The dry, sun-baked tangle of rocky slopes and gullies supporting a profusion of vegetation equipped with thorns and other armaments called for a sturdy people, and that the Apaches were; the people and the land complemented each other.

The Apaches' move westward coincided with the northward thrust of Spanish conquistadors from Mexico. By the 1700s, when the Apaches finally reached the limits of their migration, Spain had held the Rio Grande Valley for 100 years.

Like the rivers and mountains of their new homeland, the various Apache groups came to be known by names the Spaniards gave them. The Indians of Apache Pass were Chiricahuas. One of three Chiricahua groups, they roamed over much of what is now southeastern Arizona. Another band, usually called Warm Springs or Mimbres, lived to the east, among forested mountains near the Rio Grande. A third group, the Nednhis, emerged in the 1800s after some Chiricahuas took refuge in the towering wilderness of Mexico's Sierra Madre, to the south. Altogether, the Eastern, Central, and Southern Chiricahua probably numbered 1,000 to 2,000 people.

The total Apache population in the middle 1500s stood at about 8,000. On the west and northwest of the Chiricahuas were Pinals and Aravaipas. To the north lived the powerful Coyotero, or White Mountain, Apaches. Jicarillas inhabited mountains in northern New Mexico, north and east of the Spanish settlements of Santa Fe and Taos. Mescaleros occupied the Sierra Blanca and Sacramento Mountains of southern New Mexico and extended southward into Texas and Mexico.

The Chiricahua Mountains formed the homeland of the Central Chiricahua group. Trending from southeast to northwest, the mountains rise 1,000 meters* above the surrounding countryside. Pine and spruce fir forests cover the heights, while scrub oak and desert plants such as mesquite, agave, yucca, ocotillo, prickly pear, and various other cacti grow on the lower slopes. On both flanks rocky canyons plunge precipitously to the desert floor. A great stone promontory crowns the range. Viewed from a distance, it suggests a masculine face upturned to the sky and has been named "Cochise Head," in honor of the Chiricahuas' greatest chief. Nearby is a dazzling geological display known as the "wonderland of rocks," now set aside as Chiricahua National Monument. Beyond the richly grassed Sulphur Springs Valley, 48 kilometers to the west, lie the Dragoon Mountains, also a favored Chiricahua haunt and site of another rocky fantasyland, called "Cochise's Stronghold." Visible across the barren trough of the San Simon Valley, 32 kilometers east, lie the Peloncillo Mountains and the borders of the Eastern Chiricahua domain.

The Chiricahuas blended easily into this harsh land and made it support a satisfying if sometimes precarious way of life. In family bands of a dozen or more people, they moved constantly about their homeland in a perennial quest for food and as a defense measure. Although traveling in small groups, usually on foot, they could swiftly unite in larger gatherings for ceremonies or war. Dome-shaped dwellings of thatched beargrass laid on a framework of upright posts joined with willow branches, called wickiups, provided shelter. Furnishings included beds of grass and skins, woven baskets, skin containers, and utensils fashioned from bone, stone, and wood. Men wore buckskin shirts and long loincloths belted at the waist; two-piece buckskin dresses made up the woman's outfit. All sported sturdy high-topped moccasins. Thick, shoulder-length black hair and a headband instantly identified the wearer as Apache.

The land usually yielded enough food. Men hunted deer and small game, and stole horses, mules, sheep, and cattle from Mexicans and, later, from Americans. Women gathered desert foods—yucca stems, agave heads, cactus fruit, piñon nuts, berries, sunflower and other seeds, and mesquite beans. Sometimes the Chiricahuas planted corn, beans, and squash, but their nomadic habits made agriculture a minor occupation. Corn formed the base for tiswin, a weak beer of which they were very fond. Fermented mescal produced another popular beverage.

---

* As part of a National Park Service program to introduce the metric system to Americans, all measurements in this book are expressed in metric units only. At the back of the book are explanations to help you convert metric figures to customary measurements.

The camera wasn't fast enough or the boys weren't patient enough when the photographer captured these Chiricahuas playing an ancient Apache hoop and pole game.

The Geographic Setting

Apache Pass is a low, narrow saddle about 6.5 kilometers long separating the Chiricahua from the Dos Cabezas Mountains. The Dos Cabezas—Two Heads—take their name from a pair of stone domes capping the summit. Siphon Canyon, a broad sandy wash, opens an easy entrance to Apache Pass on the east, but the way to the summit is steep, tortuous, and difficult. The face of Bowie Mountain walls the pass on the south. Helen's Dome, another curious rocky promontory, is a looming landmark to the southwest. The sheer walls of the mountains tower 600 to 700 meters above the pass, which is at an elevation of 1,560 meters.

Ecologically, Apache Pass contains both lateral and vertical plant transition zones. Laterally, the Sonoran Desert flora merges with that of the Chihuahuan Desert, the latter predominating. In the vertical zone, the lower desert grasslands and shrubs intermingle with the unstructured, scattered shrubs of the chaparral community characterized by agave, yucca, sotol, beargrass, mountain mahogany, manzanita, and oak. On the higher slopes grow the open woodlands of oak and pinyon pine-juniper. The sandy drainages of the riparian woodland are shaded by such trees as walnut, hackberry, ash, bumelia, oak, willow, and cottonwood. The area of the pass is also rich in wildlife.

The pass has attracted white travelers from quite early times, for it was one of the few feasible routes through the Southwest to California. And it lay on the shortest route between Tucson and the settlements on the Rio Grande. One of the chief advantages of the pass was the Apache Springs, a de-pendable source of water in an otherwise arid land. The spring issued from a ravine that empties into Siphon Canyon.

The once vital link has been bypassed by both railroad and modern highway, and the importance men once attached to it is just a memory.

In keeping with their transitory existence, the Apaches built temporary wickiups out of whatever materials were at hand. They provided protection from the elements and a welcome place to rest as the Apaches moved about the Southwest.

Looking north from the summit of Overlook Ridge in Apache Pass you see Siphon Canyon straight ahead and the San Simon Valley to the right.

The Butterfield route in Apache Pass.

The Butterfield Overland Mail

Mail was what they wanted—and on a regular basis. As soon as the miners got to California they raised this cry, for contact with home, with the folks back east, was all-important. Petitions began to move eastward to Congress, because Californians decided that a government subsidy would be needed to pay for the overland connection between California and the rest of the country. In 1856 a petition bearing 75,000 names was laid before Congress.

The demands encountered rising sectional tensions. California wanted the route to go through South Pass which would make San Francisco—close to the Mother Lode country—the western terminus. Southerners feared that the north-central route would tie the Pacific coast to the north, thereby undoing the "balance" of slave and free states (15 slave and 16 free in 1856).

In March 1857 Congress passed a Post Office Appropriations Bill that contained provisions establishing mail service "from such point on the Mississippi River as the contractors may select, to San Francisco." No route was prescribed; that decision was left to Postmaster General Aaron V. Brown, a Tennessean. Thinking that he would choose a southern route, the Southerners had voted for the bill. Brown did not disappoint them, for he chose Memphis and St. Louis as the eastern terminals. The trails joined at Fort Smith, Ark., went to El Paso and across southern New Mexico and Arizona, then up the central valley of California to San Francisco.

Brown awarded the contract to John Butterfield and his associates on September 16, 1857. The semi-weekly service for which Butterfield would receive $600,000 annually was to begin one year from the date of the signing. In the next 12 months Butterfield built 139 stations; dug wells; bought coaches, wagons, and hundreds of horses and mules; hired station agents, drivers, and guards; contracted for hay and grain deliveries, and tied every loose end he could find. On September 15, 1858, the first eastbound coach left San Francisco. The next morning the first westward run started from St. Louis with two pouches of mail and the special correspondent for the *New York Herald,* Waterman Ormsby, who wrote six articles about his trip west. The trip took 23 days, 23½ hours from start to finish.

The Civil War made the southern portions of the overland route vulnerable and in July 1861 the route shifted north to run between St. Joseph, Mo., and Placerville, Calif. In 1869 the first transcontinental railroad was completed and mail delivery via stagecoach became obsolete and outmoded.

The Overland Mail was a brief yet colorful detail in the history of the American West. And while many believed that the service would bind the west coast to the rest of the country, the Nation was about to come apart at the seams over the slavery question.

Dispersed over a vast territory, the Chiricahuas developed no more than a loose and rudimentary political organization. They felt little tribal consciousness and never came together as a tribe. The three groups—Eastern, Central, and Southern—maintained friendly relations, respected one another's rights, and sometimes cooperated in war. Each, consisting of extended family bands, attained some cohesion and cooperative effort. Each group acknowledged a leader, and one or more of these usually exerted leadership throughout a group. Demonstrated ability and wisdom were the qualities that elevated one to group leadership, although wealth and birth also counted. Leaders were not rulers, however; they led through advice, persuasion, and example, and they served only as long as their leadership proved successful.

Befitting an outdoor people, the Chiricahuas' elaborate body of ceremony, religion, and folk belief expressed itself in the phenomena of nature—in thunder and lightning and sun and moon and stars, in animals and birds and reptiles, in trees and plants and rocks. White Painted Woman, Child of the Waters, and Killer of Enemies were precursors of a whole progeny of supernatural beings. Coyote, the ubiquitous trickster known to so many Indian tribes, was a prominent fixture in Apache lore. Religion helped one to acquire the supernatural power needed for guidance and assistance throughout life. Religion placated or nullified the evil forces that caused disease and calamity; it helped to ensure success in war. Rituals and taboos ordered almost all patterns of life. Shamans counseled the people on how to apply rituals and conducted ceremonies that gave them meaning.

Chiricahua culture emphasized warfare and awarded high distinction to successful warriors. Three central motives sustained preoccupation with war —vengeance, economics, and personal aggrandizement. Chiricahuas conducted raids to revenge themselves for the aggression of other tribes, Mexicans, or Americans; to increase their wealth by seizing horses, mules, sheep, cattle, and other plunder; and to enhance individual stature by winning war honors. Prepared from infancy, the warrior was a master of stealth, cunning, alertness, and fighting skills. He was a superb specimen of physical strength and endurance, running miles without tiring and foregoing food and water long periods of time. He was perfectly attuned to his environment, able to gain full advantage from its stark, hostile features and turn them to his foe's disadvantage. His weapons were the lance, knife, and bow and arrows. By the late 19th century, he boasted a rifle and pistol, too. He carried his arrows in a quiver of mountain lion skin slung over his shoulder and his cartridges in a heavy belt circling his waist. He knew well how to use his weapons. In all the wars for the North American continent, the European invader encountered no more formidable adversary than the Apache warrior.

Charles Schreyvogel was born in New York City in 1861. As a young man he became entranced by Buffalo Bill's Wild West Show and used the performers as the subjects of his early paintings. In his early 30s he spent several summers in the West meeting Indians and soldiers and observing the way of life that had long intrigued him.
"My Bunkie," which he painted in 1900, brought him nationwide fame. He painted "The Cavalrymen Pursued by Indians" (*above*) in 1903.

Alien Intruders

For a century or more after taking up residence in the mountains bisected by Apache Pass, the Chiricahuas enjoyed undisputed possession of their homeland. Spaniards lived in the Rio Grande Valley to the east, at Tucson and Tubac in the Santa Cruz Valley to the west, and in a scattering of villages and ranches along a frontier of settlement to the south. They gave no sign of wishing to make their homes in Apache country.

But frequently Spanish soldiers made forays into Apache country intent upon retaliation for the raids that fell so regularly and destructively upon Spanish settlements. They became familiar with the "Sierra de Chiguicagui" and with the pass that by 1766 they called, enigmatically, "Puerto del Dado"—dado meaning die, the singular of dice, which may mean that one took a chance, or gamble, in entering the pass. The Chiricahuas usually eluded such expeditions with ease, but now and then a group grew careless. One such instance, in May 1784, is typical. Soldiers attacked a small party high in the Chiricahua Mountains, killing four women and three children. "The barbarians made the most vigorous defense," reported the Spanish commander, "always taking advantage of the protection of the land, the hills and craginesses of heights and sheer pinnacles whence they unloosed and rolled rocks and fragments down on our troop."

This pattern of raid and retaliation persisted into the 19th century. It intensified after Mexico won her independence from Spain in 1821 and adopted a new mode of retaliation—the scalp bounty. Chihuahua, one of the two Mexican states that suffered most severely from Apache raids, offered $100 for a man's scalp, $50 for a woman's, and $25 for a child's. Bands of professional scalp-hunters, composed of both Mexican and American adventurers, roamed the Apache country in search of scalps. Furious, the Apaches ravaged the settlements with fresh vigor and hatred.

During Mexican rule, the Apaches became acquainted with a lighter-skinned people filtering in from the north and east. Called *norteamericanos* by the Mexicans, "white eyes" by the Apaches, they searched the Gila River and its tributaries for beaver. For the most part, the Apaches and Americans left one another alone although a brisk trade developed on the Gila River in which guns and powder were exchanged for horses and mules stolen in Mexico.

Then in 1846 the United States and Mexico went to war. The United States won, and Mexico lost her northern possessions. According to the treaty signed in 1848, the Gila River formed the boundary between the two nations in the vicinity of the Chiricahuas. The Gadsden Purchase in 1853 gave the United States a large block of territory south of the Gila. Thus the homeland of both the Eastern and Central Chiricahuas became U.S. territory.

During these middle years of the 19th century, two men gained high stature among the Chiricahuas—Mangas Coloradas ("Red Sleeves"), who belonged to the Eastern band, and Cochise of the Central. Both were "war captains," skilled in the techniques of warfare and raiding. Both were men of large and powerful physique and superior intellect. Both possessed uncommon qualities of leadership. Both were destined to play important roles in their people's early relations with the Americans who entered their homeland in growing numbers after the Mexican War.

In 1846 Mangas Coloradas greeted Gen. Stephen Watts Kearny, whose forces had seized New Mexico and were marching westward to conquer California. Mangas pledged peace and friendship to the American government. Six years later he signed a treaty. Although not above stealing stock and other plunder from New Mexican settlers, throughout the 1850s he and his warriors directed their bloodiest and most destructive forays at Mexico.

Cochise remained a shadowy figure to the Americans until late in the 1850s. He and his people watched increasing numbers of travelers cross Apache Pass, through which one of the southern transcontinental routes led. Most were emigrants, headed for California to find fortune in the gold fields. Although stealthy warriors occasionally relieved gold-seekers of stock, most travelers threaded the pass unmolested if not unobserved.

In September 1851, John Russell Bartlett, commissioned to survey the new international boundary, camped in Apache Pass without seeing any trace of Indians. Bartlett noted that the "fine spring . . . afforded the most eligible camping ground we had yet met with." In March 1854, Lts. John G. Parke and George Stoneman, surveying a route for a southern transcontinental railroad, also paused in Apache Pass. Their men mingled freely with Apaches and even bought some mules from them.

With the advent of the stagecoaches, Cochise became known to the whites

Some Apache Lore

When George Catlin, the well known painter of the American Indian, was traveling through the Chiricahua Apache country in the 1850s, he heard this Apache story of the origin of their tribe:

Their tradition is that "their tribe is the father of all existing races—that seven persons only were saved from the Deluge by ascending a high mountain, and that these seven multiplied and filled again the valleys with populations; and that those who built their villages in the valleys were very foolish, for there came a great rain which filled the valleys with water, and they were again swept away."

For a few years the Chiricahuas enjoyed peace, although they had to endure the harsh and bleak environment of the San Carlos Reservation, a situation that eventually led to another outbreak of warfare.

by name. In 1857 James Birch's San Antonio-San Diego Mail—the "Jackass Mail"—was established on a route that lay through Apache Pass. A year later the Butterfield Overland Mail supplanted Birch's line. Coaches made the 4,500-kilometer journey from Tipton, Mo., to San Francisco in 25 days. West of Apache Springs 555 meters, in the open basin where Lieutenant Parke had camped in 1854, the company built a stone stage station with living and dining quarters and, in the rear, a stone corral for mules and horses. Cochise and his people kept on friendly terms with the Butterfield agent, who paid them to supply the station with firewood.

Although Cochise professed peace and in 1859 was rewarded by the Government with a distribution of presents, warfare was a way of life not easily abandoned. Like Mangas Coloradas, however, Cochise made his most damaging raids in Mexico. Coyotero and Pinal Apaches and Yavapais showed less restraint, and Americans suffered almost as severely as Mexicans. To provide protection for the growing settlements in the Santa Cruz Valley south of Tucson, the Army in 1857 established Fort Buchanan on Sonoita Creek, a tributary of the Santa Cruz, and in 1860 planted Fort Breckinridge at the confluence of the Gila and San Pedro Rivers. Scouts, patrols, and campaigns failed to stem the Apache marauders.

The Bascom Affair

Cochise and a handful of followers were living in a canyon a few kilometers north of the Apache Pass mail station on February 3, 1861, when a company of 54 infantrymen, mounted on mules, rode into the pass from the west. Pausing briefly at the mail station, the soldiers proceeded a short distance down Siphon Canyon and made camp.

The next day Cochise, accompanied by his brother, two nephews, and a woman and two children, went to visit with the soldier chief, a youthful lieutenant named George N. Bascom. In a tense confrontation, the officer accused Cochise of stealing some horses and oxen belonging to a Sonoita Valley rancher named John Ward, and of abducting the 12-year-old son of Ward's Mexican wife. Cochise denied the accusation, charging the deed to the Coyotero instead of the Chiricahua Apaches. When Bascom declared that Cochise and his companions would be held hostage for the return of Ward's stock and the boy, the chief sprang to the wall of the tent, slit it open with his knife, and, as the startled soldiers outside fired at him, bounded up the side of the canyon. The other Apaches were swiftly made prisoners.

On February 5, Cochise and a large force of warriors, including Coyoteros under Francisco, approached the mail station under a white flag, probably to negotiate. Bascom came out under a white flag, too, but grew cautious and hesitated. Three of the station attendants, who had been friendly with Cochise, walked closer. Suddenly the Indians rushed the white men and succeeded in capturing one, James F. Wallace. The other two turned and ran amid an exchange of gunfire between soldiers and Apaches in which both of the Butterfield employees were hit, one fatally. The Indians withdrew.

That evening the Apaches seized a small freight train entering the pass from the west and thus added several more hostages—accounts differ on the number—to the one already held. The eight Mexicans with the train were bound to wagon wheels and burned with the wagons.

The next day, the sixth, Cochise made one more attempt to resolve the

George Nicholas Bascom was a second lieutenant at the time of his encounter with Cochise. Young and inexperienced, his handling of Cochise in an extremely delicate situation left much to be desired. Nevertheless he was commended by his superiors and promoted to captain within the year. He was killed at the Battle of Valverde in February 1862. Fort Bascom (now inactive) on the Canadian River in eastern New Mexico was named for him.

trouble by negotiating. With Wallace, his wrists tightly bound, Cochise met Bascom near the mail station and offered to exchange the Butterfield official and 16 stolen mules for the six Indians held by the soldiers. Bascom refused unless Ward's boy were included in the bargain—a stipulation Cochise could not meet.

Aware that both the eastbound and westbound stagecoaches were due in Apache Pass that night, Cochise made plans to ambush them. His men blocked the road in Siphon Canyon with stacks of dry grass, intending to ignite them as a means of halting the westbound coach and lighting the scene for marksmen posted on the slopes. But the coach arrived early, during the afternoon, and slipped through to safety before the warriors had taken their stations.

The eastbound coach was less fortunate. Shortly after midnight, as it entered the pass, Cochise's warriors opened fire from heights on both sides of the road, dropping the lead mule and putting a bullet in the driver's leg. The passengers cut out the dead mule and pushed on at a rapid gait. Several times they had to stop and clear the road of rocks placed there by the Indians. The Apaches had also knocked apart a stone bridge across a deep gully, leaving only the stringers. When the stage reached this point, it was moving too fast to stop. The mules leaped the gulch and the coach lurched onto the bridge with such velocity that it slid across on the axles. The wheels took hold on the opposite slope, and the coach proceeded to the mail station without further mishap.

Cochise made his next move on the morning of February 8. By now, besides his own Chiricahuas and Francisco's Coyoteros, he may well have obtained further reinforcements of Eastern Chiricahuas under Mangas Coloradas. As a detail of soldiers watered the mule herd at Apache Springs, the Indians suddenly burst from hiding and ran off with 29 mules. The soldiers pursued for about a mile and shot down a few of the quarry before calling off the chase.

Lieutenant Bascom had dispatched couriers for help. On February 10 Assistant Surgeon Bernard J. D. Irwin and an infantry escort arrived from Fort Buchanan. En route, Irwin's party had captured three Coyotero warriors who were driving stolen stock, thus adding to Bascom's hostages. Four days later two companies of dragoons under Lt. Isaiah N. Moore rode in from Fort Breckinridge.

Searching the hills, the troops found abandoned Apache camps but no Apaches. They had withdrawn into the mountains or departed altogether. Beside the road near the summit of the pass, the soldiers discovered the blackened remains of the ambushed wagon train with the charred corpses still lashed to remnants of burned wagon wheels. Finally, attracted to the north by circling vultures, the searchers came upon the bodies of Wallace and his fellow hostages, riddled with lance holes and mutilated beyond recognition. Wallace was identifiable only by the fillings in his teeth.

On February 19, as the military column made its way toward the summit of Apache Pass for the march home, the officers gathered their prisoners near the graves of the slain hostages. They spared the woman and children but hanged the six men—three Chiricahuas and three Coyoteros—from the limbs of oak trees and left their bodies dangling as a gesture of defiance and vengeance to Cochise and his people.

Before the Bascom affair, despite professions of peace and friendship, Cochise had harassed settlers and travelers with petty thievery but had never subjected them to the kind of bloodbath regularly visited upon the Mexicans. After the Bascom affair, memory of the false accusation and the execution of his kinsmen, even though in retaliation for his own excesses, aroused in him an implacable hostility toward all Americans and spurred him to wage upon them a bloody warfare that lasted for a decade.

One Man's View of the Apaches

One tends to believe that 19th-century people were uncommonly unified in their support of an Indian policy that aimed at the extermination of the race, typified by the "only-good-Indian-is-a-dead-Indian" philosophy. As is usually true, the truth of the matter cannot be so precisely defined. Jacob Piatt Dunn (1855–1924) served as librarian of the State of Indiana, controller of Indianapolis, and recording secretary of the Indiana Historical Society, and he wrote a number of books on Indiana history and politics and on Indians. These two selections from his *Massacres of the Mountains* (1886) illustrate his views that whites would inevitably dominate the land though he realized that native inhabitants would suffer:

All troubles with the Chiricahua Apaches, since 1876, resulted from an attempt to remove them from their native mountains to San Carlos Agency, an unhealthy and intolerable place for mountain Indians and occupied by bands that were unfriendly to the Chiricahuas.

It must be remembered that [Crook] had left to him a legacy of the hatred of three centuries between the peoples whom he had to pacify; that a large portion of the white population were as barbarous in their modes of warfare as the Apaches themselves; that Arizona was still a refuge for the criminal and lawless men of other states and territories; that war and pillage had been bred into the Apaches, until they were the most savage and intractable Indians in the country; that large bands of their nation still infested Northern Mexico, and had almost impregnable strongholds there; that Mexico pursued war in the old way, and still paid bounty for Apache scalps, no matter where procured; that slavery still existed in Mexico, and it was next to impossible to recover Indians once carried across the line.

The Cochise Wars

One of the passengers on the eastbound stagecoach that almost fell prey to Cochise's warriors was Lt. John Rogers Cooke, son of one of the Army's most prominent cavalry officers, Col. Philip St. George Cooke. The young officer's presence on the coach was symptomatic of a gathering storm about to break over the United States, for he was traveling east to resign his commission and offer his services to his home State, Virginia, in case war should break out.

Two months after the Bascom affair, South Carolina troops fired on Fort Sumter, and the Civil War was on. Texas troops that marched into the Rio Grande Valley above El Paso in July 1861 found the citizens sympathetic to the southern cause. The commander, Lt. Col. John R. Baylor, proclaimed all of southern New Mexico west to the Colorado River as the Confederate Territory of Arizona. The weak Federal garrisons at Forts Buchanan and Breckinridge hastily abandoned their posts and withdrew northward, beyond the range of Baylor's patrols. The Butterfield stage line had already been moved to a more northerly route. In February 1862 a Confederate cavalry company under Capt. Sherod Hunter marched west to occupy Tucson. At the same time, a full brigade of Texans under Brig. Gen. Henry H. Sibley thrust northward with the objective of seizing all New Mexico and, ultimately, Denver and the Colorado gold mines.

Knowing nothing of the great war in the East, the Apaches supposed that they had frightened the soldiers into leaving. Encouraged, they terrorized the land with robbery, pillage, and murder. Only in Tucson did white people feel safe. And Cochise all but choked off traffic at Apache Pass.

To meet the threat posed by Sibley's invasion of New Mexico, Union strategists organized a brigade of 1,800 volunteers to march eastward from California. Under Brig. Gen. James H. Carleton, a flint-eyed, hard bitten veteran of the Regular Army, the Californians occupied Tucson in May 1862.

Hunter's Confederates pulled back to the Rio Grande in the face of their advance.

In June Carleton sent out advance parties to prepare for the march to the Rio Grande. Already, Cochise's warriors had killed two couriers in Apache Pass. Later the chief and one of Carleton's officers warily exchanged greetings in Apache Pass, but that night Indians shot and lanced three soldiers who had strayed from the command and stirred a momentary turmoil by pouring a volley of musketry into the military camp.

Another advance party approached Apache Pass on July 15. With 126 men, both infantry and cavalry, a battery of two howitzers, and a large wagon train, Capt. Thomas H. Roberts had set forth from Tucson five days earlier. At Dragoon Springs he had divided his command, leaving Capt. John C. Cremony with most of the cavalry and the train while he and the infantry and artillery pushed on to see whether Apache Springs contained enough water. Among the rocks and gullies of Apache Pass, the warriors of both Cochise and Mangas Coloradas lay in wait.

At noon on July 15 the infantry marched innocently into the ambush. From above and on both sides the Apaches opened fire. Roberts quickly retreated, re-formed his command, and advanced once more into the pass. Skirmishing down the old stage road, the troops reached the abandoned Butterfield station. They could not get to water, however, for the Indians had gathered behind rock breastworks on the slopes commanding the springs. As Roberts later reported, "they seemed very loath to let me have water." He then ran his howitzers into position, and the bursting artillery shells scattered the warriors over the hill. The soldiers took possession of the springs.

Roberts sent six cavalrymen back to tell Captain Cremony that an infantry detachment would be left to hold the springs while the rest marched back to escort the wagons. No sooner had the couriers left the pass than about 40 Apaches attacked them. In a running fight Pvt. John W. Teal fell behind. A bullet dropped his horse. Taking cover behind the dying animal, Teal held the circling Indians at bay with his carbine and revolver. A well-placed shot wounded Mangas Coloradas himself, and the warriors promptly lost interest in the contest. Shouldering his saddle, Teal followed the trail of his comrades and, after a 13-kilometer hike, joined them at Cremony's new camp.

Roberts and his exhausted infantry arrived at midnight, and next morning the entire command returned to the pass. During the night the Indians had reoccupied the breastworks above the springs and again an artillery bombardment cleared them out. After digging out the springs and increasing the flow of water, the troops departed on July 17. In the two-day battle, Captain

James Henry Carleton, a flint-eyed old veteran of the Regular Army, commanded the Department of New Mexico from 1862 to 1866. His assignment was to control the Indian tribes within his jurisdiction, and he went about his job with a zeal that some critics described as ruthless. He was often accused of being arrogant, tyrannical, and a petty dictator. To others, he was a master of Indian warfare. Troops under his command broke Navajo resistance and forced that tribe on the "Long Walk" to the arid and sterile Bosque Redondo, where the Navajos' spirit was shattered.

Roberts had lost two killed and two wounded, and he reported that his men had killed nine Indians. An Apache participant later told Captain Cremony: "We would have done well enough if you had not fired wagons at us."

Reporting the Battle of Apache Pass, Captain Roberts advised General Carleton that "a force sufficient to hold the water and pass should be stationed there, otherwise every command will have to fight for water." Carleton, arriving at Apache Pass with the bulk of the Californians on July 27, agreed. As he later reported, he found it "indispensably necessary to establish a post in what is known as Apache Pass."

At the old Butterfield mail station, Carleton's adjutant wrote out the order establishing Fort Bowie, named in honor of the commander of the 5th Infantry, California Volunteers, Col. George Washington Bowie. The order specified that 100 men of Companies A and G of the 5th would remain to build the fort. Maj. T. A. Coult would superintend construction and serve as the first post commander. He would also escort travelers, mail couriers, and supply trains through the pass and "cause the Apache Indians to be attacked whenever and wherever he may find them near his post." The next day, July 28, 1862, Fort Bowie officially came to life.

Completed in two and one-half weeks, the new fort looked more like a temporary camp than a permanent installation. It sprawled on a hill domi-

George Washington Bowie,
colonel of the 5th California Infantry,
was the man for whom Fort Bowie
was named.

nating the springs. On the four faces of this hill the Californians built defensive outworks. As Coult described them:

> The total length of wall around the post is 412 feet, the height four to four and a half feet, and thickness from two and a half to three feet at bottom, tapering to eighteen inches to two feet at top, and built of stones weighing from twenty-five to 500 pounds. The works are not of any regular form, my only object being to build defenses which could be speedily completed, and at the same time possess the requisites of sheltering their defenders, commanding every approach to the hill, and protecting each other by flank fires along their faces.

The breastworks enclosed canvas tents in which the men lived, as well as a stone guardhouse equipped with firing ports.

Even though a makeshift creation, Fort Bowie, Coult believed, would serve its purpose. It did. Officers and men alike regarded it as an exceedingly undesirable station even after a larger and more substantial post was built. But despite any discomforts, the post was effective and the Chiricahuas never again controlled Apache Pass.

By the time Carleton reached the Rio Grande, General Sibley's Confederates had been defeated and driven back to Texas by Volunteer troops from

The first Fort Bowie was a ramshackle collection of stone and adobe huts scattered across the hillside. It was enough, however, to guarantee control of the pass and its water supply.

Colorado. For the remaining years of the Civil War, therefore, the Californians joined New Mexico Volunteers in fighting Indians in both New Mexico and the Territory of Arizona, which was carved out of western New Mexico in 1863.

One of the Californians' first blows fell on Mangas Coloradas. After the Battle of Apache Pass, a Mexican doctor had been forced to remove Teal's carbine bullet from the chief's chest. Six months later he was back home, harassing miners at the Piños Altos gold mines, near modern Silver City, N.M. Some of Carleton's troops lured him into their grasp with a white flag and made him prisoner. That night, as the military report described it, Mangas "made three efforts to escape and was shot on the third attempt." A prospector who was present later disclosed that the "efforts to escape" had been provoked by heated bayonets applied to Mangas' bare feet.

The death of Mangas merely confirmed Cochise in his bitterness and he led his warriors in raids that spared no American or Mexican unlucky enough to fall within his grasp. Murders and depredations multiplied, and citizens and officials cried in vain for enough troops to subjugate the Apaches.

Almost alone, the tiny garrison at Fort Bowie stood against Cochise's tribesmen. Although the troops successfully carried out Carleton's instruc-

At the time of its abandonment in 1894, Fort Bowie was a full-fledged post. A new hospital had just been completed on the far slope behind the commanding officer's home. Large cottonwood trees, carefully tended and watered in the arid climate, flourished in front of the officers' homes around the parade ground.

Just 20 years after abandonment, the fort had almost been stripped bare. All windows, doors, and roofs had been salvaged by inhabitants of the area. The cottonwoods had withered away and died.

Fort Bowie Ariz
1894

Reuben Bernard, a native of East
Tennessee, enlisted in the U.S. Army
a few years before the Civil War
broke out. He remained in the U.S.
Army and served in the West.
Later, as a captain in the 1st
Cavalry, he commanded Fort
Bowie in the last stages of the
Cochise wars, 1869-71. Bernard
went on to become a general. He is
shown here about 1890 nearing the
close of a professional career marked
by 101 combat actions against
Indians and Civil War Confederates.

tions to protect that part of his line of communication lying through Apache
Pass, they found it impossible to "cause the Apache Indians to be attacked
whenever and wherever" they might be found. Rarely did the fort hold more
than 100 men; 50 was the usual complement. Such a small force could do
little more than garrison the post and provide escort service through the pass.
Occasional patrols sought to ferret out the Indians, but with scant success.

Fort Bowie afforded its occupants few of even the most basic comforts.
Describing the fort in 1863, an officer wrote to Carleton:

> The quarters, if it is not an abuse of language to call them such, have
> been constructed without system, regard to health, defense or convenience.
> Those occupied by the men are mere hovels, mostly excavations in the
> side hill, damp, illy ventilated, and covered with decomposed granite taken
> from the excavation, through which the rain passes very much as it would
> through a sieve. By the removal of a few tents, the place would present
> more the appearance of a California digger rancheria than a military post.

Isolation, bad food, and widespread sickness added to the misery. And if Indians were seldom seen they were nevertheless present, making vigilance the
price of life. To sustain morale, Carleton frequently rotated the garrison.
Not until more than a year after the close of the Civil War were the Cali-

fornia Volunteers discharged. On May 3, 1866, Capt. W. H. Brown arrived at Fort Bowie with Company E, 14th U.S. Infantry.

The Regulars boasted no greater strength than had the Volunteers, but in 1868 they enlarged the fort and made it less primitive. A new location was selected on a plateau southeast of the first fort, and construction of adobe quarters began at once. Substantial barracks, a row of houses for officers, corrals and storehouses, a post trader's store, and a commodious hospital soon occupied the four sides of the sloping parade ground. In subsequent years more buildings were added. At the time of its abandonment in 1894, Fort Bowie consisted of some three dozen structures, most of them of adobe and milled timbers.

In 1866 mail service resumed between El Paso and Tucson. A post office opened at Fort Bowie, and mail carriers rode through Apache Pass twice a week. Cochise's warriors ambushed some carriers. Whenever one was killed patrols normally set out in pursuit, but rarely did they catch the offenders.

In 1869 an unusually able officer took command of Fort Bowie. As a dragoon sergeant, Reuben F. Bernard had ridden with the Fort Breckinridge column to Lieutenant Bascom's relief in 1861. Now as captain of Troop G, 1st Cavalry, Bernard returned to Apache Pass to lead a series of aggressive expeditions against Cochise. In October 1869 he and 61 men fought a battle with Apaches in the Chiricahua Mountains and killed 18 warriors. A week later he encountered Cochise again and, after a hard fight, found himself and his troops surrounded and forced to fortify his position. A relief party from Bowie failed to break the siege, and only when a strong force from Camp Crittenden approached did the Apaches scatter into the mountains. Early in 1870 Bernard retaliated by surprising his foes in the Dragoon Mountains and killing 13. Again in January 1871 Bernard struck. He fell on a hostile camp in the Pinal Mountains, killed nine Indians, and wounded many more.

Much of the same pattern of conflict prevailed throughout Arizona as other Apaches followed Cochise's example. The Regulars strove to meet this challenge and established more forts—Crittenden, Grant, Lowell, Verde, McDowell, and Apache. Each provided a base for the kind of small-unit operations that Captain Bernard mounted at Bowie. But despite dozens of battles and skirmishes, hostilities dragged on year after year.

In 1871, to breathe new life into a lagging military effort, the Army assigned a new commander to the Department of Arizona. Although a junior lieutenant colonel, George Crook had demonstrated in recent campaigns against tribes in Idaho and Oregon that, unlike most Regular Army officers,

Oliver Otis Howard

Oliver Otis Howard is one of those persons who doesn't quite fit any stereotype. By profession he was a military man. By choice he was a humanitarian. And throughout his entire life ran a river of idealism that tempered every act. He was a complex man who probably had more than his fair share of admirers *and* critics.

Howard was born November 8, 1830, in Leeds, Maine. After graduation from Bowdoin College in 1850, he entered West Point and graduated four years later, fourth in his class. When the Civil War broke out he began active service as a colonel in the 3d Maine Regiment. He lost his right arm at Fair Oaks, Va., and in 1893 Congress gave him the Medal of Honor for his courage in that battle. Though his personal bravery was never questioned, controversy surrounded his decisions and judgments during the battles of Chancellorsville and Gettysburg. In 1864 he was promoted to brigadier general in the Regular Army.

At the end of the war, President Andrew Johnson appointed him commissioner of the Freedmen's Bureau. In enthusiasm and passion Howard was a choice without peer, but as an executive and administrator he was sorely lacking. He failed to see that his subordinates were inept and corrupt and would not tolerate criticism of his staff. He thereby effectively undermined the workings of the Bureau and soon exhausted the reservoir of goodwill that the Bureau had originally had.

Howard was instrumental in founding Howard University, which was named for him, and served as its first president from 1869 to 1874. In the mid-1870s he returned to active military life and participated mostly in the Indian Wars, fighting against the Apaches, Nez Perce, the Bannocks, and Paiutes. From 1880–82 he was superintendent of West Point and in 1886 he was promoted to major general. Eight years later he retired.

George Crook (1829–1890) was quietly
unorthodox. He donned a uniform to
sit for this photograph but rarely wore one
either in the office or in the field. He
preferred a shotgun to a rifle and a mule
to a horse. And his views on the treatment
of Indians were out of step with the times.
He believed that Indians and whites would
both benefit if the Indians were granted
equality before the law and given all the
privileges of citizenship.

he understood the conditions of war with a foe that did not fight in the or-
thodox manner.

Crook's first objective was "to iron all the wrinkles out of Cochise's
band." In the midst of a familiarization tour of Fort Bowie and other posts,
however, he learned that the administration of President Ulysses S. Grant
had decided to test its highly touted "Peace Policy" in Arizona. Disgusted,
Crook suspended his plans while emissaries of the President attempted the
new approach of "conquest by kindness."

The first two peace emissaries, Gen. Gordon Granger and Vincent Colyer,
failed to make a settlement with Cochise. A third then tried. He was Brig.
Gen. Oliver O. Howard, a one-armed veteran of the Civil War on loan to
the Interior Department. His deep and prominently displayed piety led
Crook to view him as a pompous religious fanatic. But Howard was wholly
committed to the Peace Policy. While Crook chafed at the delay of his campaign, Howard made one unsuccessful effort after another to open communication with Cochise.

Finally, Howard chanced upon an army scout named Thomas J. Jeffords.

Taken late in life at his Arizona ranch, this photograph reflects the peaceful ways of Tom Jeffords, who, alone, rode into Cochise's territory and made friends with the Chiricahua chief and later helped pave the way for peace.

In 1867 Jeffords had superintended the mail service between Fort Bowie and Tucson but had resigned in disgust over the Army's inability to protect his mail riders. As a prospector, he had then worked out an arrangement with Cochise personally that earned him immunity from Chiricahua war parties and laid the basis for a lifelong friendship. Jeffords consented to guide Howard to Cochise's stronghold in the Dragoon Mountains if no military escort went along. Howard agreed to this condition.

The party that rode westward across the Sulphur Springs Valley late in September 1872 consisted only of Howard and his aide, Jeffords, and two Chiricahuas. Repeatedly, they kindled a ring of five fires on the prairie to indicate that five people came in peace. What their reception would be, neither Jeffords nor the Apache guides would guess. One evening two Indian boys appeared at Howard's bivouac and led the party to a secluded mountain valley that hid an Apache camp. Next morning Cochise, accompanied by his brother, son, and two wives rode into the camp. "This is the man," whispered Jeffords to Howard. The general waited apprehensively. Cochise dismounted, embraced Jeffords warmly, then turned to Howard, grasped his hand, and said, "Buenos dias, Señor."

Peace With Cochise and the Chiricahuas

Sitting on the ground, Cochise and Howard began to talk. For ten days Howard stayed in the village, bargaining with Cochise about the settlement. Cochise recited the many wrongs done him by the whites, dwelling with particular bitterness on the Bascom affair. Still, he declared, he wanted peace. The general outlined a plan for forming a reservation for all Apaches, including the Chiricahuas, on the Rio Grande. Cochise replied that he liked the Rio Grande country but that many Chiricahuas did not. To accept such a reservation would badly divide his people. Instead, he asked: "Why not give me Apache Pass? I will see that nobody's property is taken by Indians."

While the two men talked, subchiefs straggled in from distant camps to join the parley. Eventually Howard bowed to Cochise's wish to remain in his home country and proposed a reservation embracing a large part of the Chiricahua Mountains and the adjoining Sulphur Springs and San Simon Valleys. But even this proposal prompted dispute, and Howard waited in suspense as the Chiricahua leaders argued. Finally Cochise gave their answer. "Hereafter," he said, "the white man and the Indian are to drink of the same water, eat of the same bread, and be at peace."

Although incensed at Howard's interference with the projected offensive against the Chiricahuas and skeptical of Cochise's sincerity, Crook had no choice but to honor the peace settlement. He turned his attention to the Tonto Basin of central Arizona, the rugged haunt of marauding bands of Yavapais and some Apaches. In the historic campaign of 1872–73, he brought about the surrender of most of the hostile groups and concentrated them on a reservation at Camp Verde. Peace came to Arizona. President Grant rewarded Crook with promotion to brigadier general.

To the great delight of the Chiricahuas, General Howard had Tom Jeffords named as their agent. A realist, Jeffords recognized that his charges had not been conquered and would continue to do just about as they

Howard Meets Cochise

Years after General Howard's meeting with Cochise, Howard wrote a children's book about the incident. This passage from *Famous Indian Chiefs I Have Known* describes the initial confrontation:

We had just had our breakfast when the chief [Cochise] rode in. He wore a single robe of stout cotton cloth and a Mexican sombrero on his head with eagle feathers on it. With him were his sister and his wife, Natchee, his son, about fourteen years old, and Juan, his brother, besides other Indians. When he saw us he sprang from his horse and threw his arms about Jeffords and embraced him twice, first on one side, then on the other. When Jeffords told him who I was, he turned to me in a gentlemanly way, holding out his hand and saying: "Buenos dias, señor." He greeted us all pleasantly and asked us to go to the council ground where the chief Indians had already gathered. . . .

Ponce and Chie first told Cochise all about me, who I was, and what I had done for other Indians. He seemed very pleased with the story, and you may be sure we watched very carefully to see how he took it. I answered him plainly that the President had sent me to make peace with him. He replied: "Nobody wants peace more than I do. I have killed ten white men for every Indian I have lost, but still the white men are no less, and my tribe keeps growing smaller and smaller, till it will disappear from the face of the earth if we do not have a good peace soon."

Cochise on Peace

During the 1871 negotiations that ultimately failed, Cochise made a statement of his hopes to Gen. Gordon Granger:

Now that I am cool I have come with my hands open to you to live in peace with you. I speak straight and do not wish to deceive or be deceived. I want a good, strong and lasting peace. When God made the world he gave one part to the white man and another to the Apache. Why was it? Why did they come together? Now, that I am to speak, the sun, the moon, the earth, the air, the waters, the birds and beasts, even the children unborn shall rejoice at my words. . . . I do not wish to hide anything from you nor have you hide anything from me; I will not lie to you; do not lie to me. I want to live in these mountains; I do not want to go to Tularosa. That is a long ways off. The flies on those mountains eat out the eyes of the horses. The bad spirits live there. I have drunk of these waters and they have cooled me. I do not want to leave here.

Natchez, Cochise's son, tried to hold the tribe together after his father's death and to follow the peaceful goals of Cochise and Jeffords. Eventually despair and frustration overcame his intentions and he became a steadfast member of Geronimo's band, staying with him until the final surrender.

pleased. But he also believed that, as long as he issued rations and did not interfere in their affairs, they would keep the peace. Cochise worked quietly with the agent to make reservation life succeed. The friendship between the two and the chief's great powers of leadership kept the Indians under restraint. Arizona settlers voiced amazement that Cochise actually kept his word. In Arizona he did keep the peace, but in Mexico he did not. For generations Chiricahuas had raided in Mexico, and they did not intend to stop now simply because they had a reservation and an agent.

Early in 1874 Cochise fell ill, and on June 8 he died. The Chiricahuas selected his son, Taza, as their new chief. Taza worked closely with Jeffords to carry forward the peaceful policy cemented by Cochise and Howard. But Taza lacked his father's force and vision, and increasingly the Chiricahuas drifted without the strong leadership on which the outcome of the reservation experiment depended.

Twice between 1872 and 1876 Jeffords moved the agency, the place where rations and supplies were distributed. Howard had placed it at Sulphur Springs. In September 1873, in search of better land for farming, Jeffords moved it across the Chiricahua Mountains to San Simon. After only two months, malaria forced abandonment of this location in favor of another, in Pinery Canyon southwest of Fort Bowie. Convenient to Apache Pass, the Chiricahua men soon learned that travelers and freighters would trade whisky for horses, a transaction agreeable to both parties but demoralizing to the Indians. In an attempt to control this commerce, Jeffords moved the agency again, in the summer of 1875, and established himself in Apache Pass near Fort Bowie.

Friction with his superiors increasingly troubled Jeffords. The Indian Bureau wanted the Indians governed rigidly, made self-supporting, and started on the road to "civilization." Jeffords knew such aims to be visionary and continued the loose management he had adopted in 1872. The Indian Bureau withheld cooperation and support. At times Jeffords had to buy supplies for the Indians with his own money. The Bureau also disliked the location of the Chiricahua Reservation. Resting on the international boundary, it not only encouraged and facilitated Chiricahua raids into Mexico but also attracted other Apaches who used it as a base for their own raids. And the Bureau had a new policy of bringing all Apaches together on a single reservation, San Carlos, in the parched bottoms of the Gila River some 121 kilometers to the north. By 1876, officials in Washington merely awaited an excuse both to rid themselves of Jeffords and to move the Chiricahuas to San Carlos.

President Grant's Peace Policy

Jurisdictional disputes, humanitarian interests, charges of corruption, and countercharges of butchery all combined to make controversy the most constant aspect of Indian policy in the first decade after the Civil War.

In the mid-1860s government officials established four principles, which they planned to use for dealing with all Indian tribes. The principles were: 1. concentration (putting all Indians on reservations and keeping them there), 2. education, 3. civilization, and 4. agricultural self-help. In other words, the Indians would be assimilated into society on the white man's terms.

Problems arose almost immediately because of confusion between the areas of civil and military control. Whenever trouble developed, the Army was called in, but once peace was restored the civil authorities took control. The Army argued that everyone's interests would be served best if the confusion of dual authority were eliminated. Of course, the Army meant that all control should come within its purview. The Indian Bureau protested that nothing in the Army's record could assure a policy of fairness and justice to the Indians. The Army in turn charged that the Indian Bureau was so riddled with corruption that any change would be for the better. So matters stood when Ulysses Grant assumed the Presidency in March 1869.

The Army believed that Grant would support its views and transfer the Indian Bureau to Army control. Grant, however, decided to try a mixture of all the proposals that faced him. The collective result came to be known as "Grant's Peace Policy." Agents and superintendents would be nominated by church representatives. In practice, only a few of these positions were filled by Quakers, while most of the rest were Army officers temporarily assigned to the Indian Bureau. The Army was to have authority over all Indians off the reservations and the Indian Bureau over all those on the reservations. On the surface this appeared to solve the problem of overlapping jurisdictions. But before the theory could be carried out, events on the northern Plains altered the application of the new policy.

In January 1870 troops under Maj. Eugene Baker attacked a village of Piegan Blackfeet. Humanitarians charged that Baker's action was unprovoked, and the question of the military role in Indian affairs was once again raised.

During the next four years the Peace Policy enjoyed varying degrees of success and failure. Gen. O. O. Howard successfully made peace with Cochise and his band of Chiricahua Apaches. The Quaker superintendents established a reputation for honesty, integrity, and fairness in dealing with the Indians. Unfortunately the Indians had come to expect the worst when dealing with the white man and often took advantage of the Quakers. The Indians also became more restive as they began to sense the approaching end of their way of life. The Modoc War in northern California in 1873 and the advent of the Red River War the next year dealt fatal blows to the Peace Policy. Peaceful methods, admittedly only halfheartedly applied and always under attack, had not worked.

The Apaches themselves provided the excuse. Because of short rations in the spring of 1876, Jeffords let the Indians hunt in the Dragoon Mountains. While camped there, they fell to quarreling. Taza took most of the people back to Apache Pass, but Skinya and about 12 families remained in the Dragoon Mountains. While intoxicated, Skinya's brother, Pionsenay, killed two of his sisters, then killed a whisky-seller and his partner when denied more whisky. With other malcontents, Pionsenay next embarked on a raid in the San Pedro Valley. Soldiers from Fort Bowie failed to catch the outlaws.

At once Jeffords declared all Indians west of the Chiricahua Mountains hostile—Pionsenay and his followers—but the damage had been done. The governor of Arizona Territory denounced all Chiricahuas and their agent and demanded their removal. The Indian Bureau reacted promptly. Early in May the agent at San Carlos, John P. Clum, received orders to go to Apache Pass, suspend Jeffords, and move the Chiricahuas. He called for military help, and the department commander, Gen. August V. Kautz, who had succeeded Crook in 1875, placed 10 troops of cavalry at Fort Bowie.

Aware of the Government's plans, the Chiricahuas held a council on the night of June 4. Skinya and Pionsenay demanded that the Chiricahuas again go to war against the whites. Taza and Natchez, younger son of Cochise, argued for peace and submission. A fight broke out in which Skinya was killed and Pionsenay and Taza wounded. Only the arrival of soldiers from Fort Bowie averted further bloodshed.

When Clum reached Fort Bowie, he called a council with the Indians and explained the reasons for the Government's action. Taza agreed to the removal, and on June 12 Clum and 325 Chiricahuas, escorted by General Kautz's soldiers, left Fort Bowie for San Carlos. The Chiricahua Reservation was promptly restored to the public domain.

This simple wooden grave marker in the Fort Bowie cemetery summons up thoughts of the old west and of an era gone by. Incidentally, the photograph was taken in 1893 by Owen Wister, author of *The Virginian*.

Geronimo and Crook

Not all the Chiricahuas followed Taza to San Carlos. Some went to Mexico and joined with the Nednhi Chiricahuas who lived in the lofty, almost inaccessible Sierra Madre. To the whites these Indians were "renegades." Free of the restraints imposed by Jeffords and the reservation, they once more began to strike at the Arizona settlements. The principal chief of the Nednhis was Juh. But increasingly they also honored a scowling, thick-set warrior whose feats had already made his name a cause for terror in Mexico: Geronimo.

For three years, 1876–79, General Kautz and his successor, Gen. Orlando B. Willcox, directed operations against these elusive raiders. Troops from Fort Bowie and the newly founded Camp Huachuca, to the west, took to the field. They scoured the Chiricahua and Dragoon Mountains, skirmishing frequently with the Indians but only occasionally fighting seriously.

Especially active in these operations were two able young officers stationed at Fort Bowie, Lts. Austin Henely and John A. Rucker. In January 1877 Rucker led 52 soldiers and 34 Indian scouts in an attack on a hostile camp in New Mexico's Liedendorf Mountains. The Indians lost 10 men killed, a number wounded, and all their camp equipage and stock. The next December Rucker again engaged a band in New Mexico and inflicted even greater damage. Meanwhile, Lieutenant Henely extensively scouted the country west and south of Fort Bowie.

The vigorous operations of the team of Rucker and Henely came to a tragic end in the summer of 1878. Near Camp Supply, in the mountains south of Fort Bowie, Henely was trying to cross a flooded canyon when the torrent swept him under. Rucker tried to save him, but drowned in the effort Both were buried in the post cemetery at Fort Bowie on July 13, and the name of the supply base was changed from Camp Supply to Camp John A. Rucker.

Military campaigns continued for another year. Finally, late in 1879, Geronimo and Juh, largely through the efforts of Tom Jeffords and Lt. H. L. Haskell, surrendered. With 105 followers, they arrived at Fort Bowie on December 29. A week later they were escorted to San Carlos and settled on the reservation.

For two years the Chiricahuas remained at peace. In fact, except for the fugitives in Mexico, most of the Chiricahuas had lived quietly on the San Carlos Reservation since their removal in 1876. They had dug a network of irrigation ditches and grew wheat, barley, and corn. Taza had died during a trip to Washington, D.C., and Geronimo and Natchez, Taza's younger brother, gained stature among the people.

The San Carlos Reservation was not a pleasant place to live. The Gila River Valley was hot, barren, and disease-ridden. Corrupt agents diverted Indian goods for their own enrichment and proved otherwise unfit for their assignment. Intrigue and factionalism caused tension in both the Indian and white communities. Intertribal friction, the result of historic rivalries, threatened the peace. White settlers circled the reservation and in places encroached on it.

As conditions worsened, unrest spread through the various Apache groups confined to the reservation. Especially affected were the Coyotero Apaches, who lived in the mountains north of the Gila, near Fort Apache. They fell under the influence of a medicine man named Nakaidoklini, whose mystical teachings and prophecies created great excitement.

On August 30, 1881, a military detachment from Fort Apache led by Col. Eugene A. Carr tried to arrest Nakaidoklini at his home on Cibicue Creek. Fighting broke out and a soldier killed the medicine man. Carr's Indian scouts mutinied and killed their captain. Coyotero warriors surrounded the troops, but under cover of darkness they slipped out of the trap.

The Battle of Cibicue alarmed Arizonans. The Army poured fresh troops into the area and quickly put down the uprising. Their presence, however, badly upset the Chiricahuas, who feared that they might suffer for the offenses of the Coyoteros. On September 30, 74 Chiricahuas, including Juh, Geronimo, and Natchez, fled the reservation and headed for Mexico. Despite efforts to cut them off, they made good their escape. Troops from Fort Bowie, once more commanded by Captain Bernard, joined others patrolling the border to keep raiding parties out of the United States.

The Chiricahuas remained in the Sierra Madre all winter, sniping at Mexican settlements but ignoring the United States. Then in April 1882 a war party under Juh, Geronimo, and Natchez slipped through the screen of cavalry and struck at Arizona settlements. At San Carlos they forced Loco, an

Geronimo, known to his followers as Goyathlay, was born in southern Arizona in June 1829. In his early days he rode with Cochise, Mangas Coloradas, and Victorio. It was not until the Chiricahuas were moved to the San Carlos Reservation and frustration with the reservation system began to mount that Geronimo began to emerge as the leader of the malcontents. For ten years he led his small band against overwhelming odds, finally suffering defeat and imprisonment.

The government sought to concentrate all Apaches on the San Carlos Reservation in the parched, furnace-like Gila River Valley in hopes of better controlling their wanderings. The Apache Wars of the 1880s broke out when "renegades" rebelled against the intolerable restraints and left the reservation for Mexico, hopeful of one day returning to their homeland in the cool, well-watered heights of the Chiricahua Mountains.

influential chief, and more Chiricahuas to join in hostilities. Now numbering 700, the fugitive band raced southward toward the Mexican sanctuary. Col. George A. Forsyth intercepted them at Horseshoe Canyon, in the Peloncillo Mountains, but they escaped. Another command, under Capt. T. C. Tupper, got on the trail too. Both Forsyth and Tupper followed the Apaches into Mexico. Preoccupied with fighting off their pursuers, the Indians fell into an ambush prepared by Mexican troops and in a bloody fight lost about 100 people. The rest scattered into the Sierra Madre.

General Willcox had shown little aptitude for contending with Apaches. The April raid convinced authorities in Washington that a new commander was needed. On September 4, 1882, General Crook again assumed command of the Department of Arizona.

First Crook set about reorganizing the administration of San Carlos Reservation. In November he called the reservation Indians into council and explained the new system. No longer would they have to live near the agency and report frequently for roll call. Henceforth they could settle wherever on the reservation they chose. Now that they could seek out better land, Crook told them, they would be expected to make a serious attempt at farming and self-support. Although the civilian agent and his staff would still perform their duties, the Indians would also be accountable to military agents—Capt. Emmet Crawford at San Carlos and Lt. Charles B. Gatewood at Fort Apache. These officers would recruit and command companies of Indian scouts to enforce the peace.

Next Crook turned to the Chiricahuas in the Sierra Madre. His previous tour in Arizona had convinced him that it took an Apache to catch an Apache. Regular troops were too slow and cumbersome for the mountain-and-desert warfare at which the Apaches excelled. He therefore reorganized the Apache scout corps and recruited it to full strength. Skilled frontiersmen who had served Crook in the past turned up to enlist as scouts. Among them were Al Sieber, Sam Bowman, and Archie McIntosh. The leading advocate of packmules for supply transport, Crook devoted careful attention to organizing his trains. Under his veteran packmaster, Tom Moore, they were brought to peak efficiency.

While Crook prepared, the raiders struck again. In March 1883 Chato and 25 warriors crossed the border. In six days, despite frantic efforts by troops from Fort Bowie and other outposts, the Apaches blazed a bloody trail across southern Arizona, killing about a dozen white people and disappearing into Mexico without being sighted by a single soldier.

General Crook did not present a very dashing figure on a mule, but he did know that these animals were far better suited than horses to the terrain in which he was working. Here he is astride his favorite mule "Apache."

Two of Crook's most trusted officers were Capt. Emmet Crawford (*left*) and Lt. Charles Gatewood (*right*). Crawford was killed deep in Mexico by Mexican militia who were unsure of the American's identity. Gatewood induced Geronimo to surrender to General Miles, but other officers received the credit and promotions.

For Crook, Chato's raid yielded an unexpected benefit. One of the raiders, Tzoe, deserted, surrendered at San Carlos, and agreed to lead Crook to the Chiricahua camps in Mexico. The soldiers, noting his light complexion, promptly dubbed the Indian "Peaches."

Having wrung reluctant permission from the Mexican Government for U.S. troops to enter Mexico in pursuit of hostile Indians, Crook crossed the border early in May 1883 with 193 Apache scouts under Captain Crawford and a troop of the Sixth Cavalry under Capt. Adna R. Chaffee. Guided by Peaches, the expedition marched to the headwaters of the Yaqui River. From there Crawford's scouts combed the rugged mountain wilderness. On May 15 they surprised Chato's camp, but the Apaches scattered into the mountains with few casualties. Three days later, however, Chihuahua appeared at Crook's camp to confer with the general. One by one, Geronimo, Chato, Natchez, and others followed. Juh had been killed in an accident and Geronimo now seemed to be the leader to whom the others looked for guidance.

That the mountains of Mexico no longer offered a secure haven had come as a revelation to the Indians. They declared their readiness to be forgiven and return to the reservation. Crook curtly informed them that he was not especially anxious to make peace. Mexican forces, he said, were even then closing in on the Apache stronghold and would probably solve the Apache

With packmules, Crook's men could follow the Indians anywhere they went.

A Tombstone photographer, C.S. Fly, accompanied Crook's Sierra Madre expedition of 1886 and photographed Crook (*seated, center, in sun helmet*), officers, scouts, and packers in camp before crossing the international boundary into Mexico.

Geronimo's band was never large. Here C.S. Fly has photographed a few of them in their camp during the 1886 campaign led by Crook.

Geronimo and Natchez, on horseback, provided skilled leadership that overcame the numerical superiority of the U.S. Army.

Tzoe, nicknamed Peaches by the soldiers, defected from Geronimo's band during Chato's raid through Arizona in 1883 and became an Apache Scout for the U.S. Army. He led Crook to the Apache stronghold in Mexico's Sierra Madre. That the Army now had access to Geronimo's hiding places was a serious blow to his continued resistance.

Chato's six-day raid through Arizona in March 1883 dramatized to the white settlers the continuing menace of the Apache fugitives who had been driven out of their homeland into Mexico.

A cavalry troop moves out on patrol from Fort Bowie in the 1880s. In the background is the back of the post trader's store.

problem by killing all the Apaches. With a show of reluctance, however, he finally consented to accept the surrender. Escorted by Crawford and his scouts, 325 Chiricahuas arrived at San Carlos on June 24.

Not all the Indians, however, had accompanied Crawford to San Carlos. Some, in fact, had tarried in Mexico on the pretext that their widely scattered bands would have to be assembled. They had promised to report at the agency in "two moons." Five moons, or months, later they had not appeared, and Arizona newspapers scored Crook for failure. In October 1883, therefore, Crook ordered Lt. Britton Davis and his scout company to find the procrastinating Chiricahuas and return them to the reservation. Camping near the border, Davis sent scouts into Mexico. Finally, Natchez and Zele brought their people in and Davis, assisted by troops from Fort Bowie, escorted them to the reservation. In January 1884 he returned, found Chato and Mangas (son of Mangas Coloradas), and took them to the agency.

Only Geronimo remained out now. For a third time, Davis camped on the border. Six weeks of scouting at last brought Geronimo and his band, trailing a herd of 350 cattle stolen from Mexican ranchers, to Davis' camp. On the way to San Carlos, a U.S. marshal and a posse of deputized cowboys tried to arrest Geronimo and take him to Tucson for civil trial. Aided by a West Point classmate from Fort Bowie, however, Davis tricked the marshal and eluded the posse. With Geronimo safely settled at San Carlos, the Apaches once more were all at peace.

For two years Arizona again enjoyed a respite from Apache depredations. On the reservation, however, the Chiricahuas found themselves caught in a power struggle between their military and civil agents. On July 7, 1883, the Secretaries of War and Interior had signed a joint memorandum giving General Crook police control of all the Indians on the San Carlos Reservation. The agreement merely perpetuated the curse of divided authority. When the military agents, Captain Crawford and Lieutenant Gatewood, attempted to extend their authority over the Apaches, the civilian administrators resisted. Sensing the conflict, the Indians sought to play off their overseers against one another. They openly defied the prohibition against beating their wives and drinking tizwin.

Conditions went from bad to worse after the transfer of Crawford and Gatewood to other stations. The climax came on May 15, 1885. After a defiant tizwin drunk, Geronimo, Natchez, Chihuahua, Mangas, and old Nana, accompanied by 42 warriors and 92 women and children, bolted the reservation and once again struck for Mexico. Soldiers from Forts Bowie, Thomas, Huachuca, and Grant enacted the familiar ritual of spreading out to inter-

Apache Scouts line up for a photograph at Fort Grant in 1886.

The Apache Scouts

Using Indians to track down and fight other Indians was not a new idea. The English and French from early colonial times had exploited traditional intertribal rivalries to their own advantage. What was novel in this case was using an Indian against members of his own tribe. This was the work of George Crook who firmly believed that the best work would be done by an Indian who had only just recently been fighting him. "The nearer an Indian approached to the savage state," Crook said, "the more likely he will prove valuable as a soldier." Crook had learned that such a scout would be a veritable well of information, for he would intimately know the fighting habits, the hiding places, and the personalities of the Indians being pursued. This method worked well for Crook and by the end of his career he had used about 500 Apache scouts.

Crook demanded loyalty from his troops and in turn he gave them his trust. He paid his scouts well and on time, a very important factor. He did not demean or abuse them. Though all these qualities no doubt earned Crook the admiration of his Indian soldiers, the man himself won their respect. Crook was like few West Point trained officers, for as one man who served under Crook wrote, "there never was an officer in our military service so completely in accord with all the ideas, views, and opinions of the savages whom he had to fight or control as was General Crook. In time of campaign this knowledge placed him, as it were, in the secret councils of the enemy. . . ." He learned to fight the Indians on their terms, to use the land and terrain to his advantage, and to abandon the textbook examples. He got on a trail and, with his Apache scouts to guide him, he followed his quarry relentlessly.

Crook's faith in his scouts never wavered. And they gave him no grounds for worry. In the annals of the Indian Wars, the story of Crook and his scouts is unique.

Seated, second from left, with some of his officers is Maj. Eugene Beaumont, who commanded Fort Bowie in 1886 during the final stages of the operations against Geronimo.

Major Beaumont complained of "the large amount of useless and unnecessary ornamentation" in his quarters. But by Victorian standards the decoration was moderate. Besides the restrained approach, the plethora of potted plants and palms so necessary to the Victorian parlor is missing, no doubt victim of the arid climate.

What brought these officers and their ladies out to pose for the photographer in front of the commanding officer's quarters in 1885? Perhaps it was just a lazy Sunday afternoon, and they were all dressed up and had no place to go.

A comfortable chair in the cooling shade of a grape vine—what could be more inviting for an afternoon nap?

cept the fugitives. But the Apaches easily evaded their pursuers and vanished into the Sierra Madre.

Lt. Gen. Philip H. Sheridan, the Army's commander, ordered an immediate offensive to round up the escapees. On June 9 he wired Crook authority to enlist an additional 200 Indian scouts and instructed him to establish headquarters on or near the newly completed Southern Pacific Railroad. Crook chose Fort Bowie, which was 21 kilometers south of Bowie Station and also convenient to the field of operations. On June 11 he arrived at the fort. From that day until the final surrender of Geronimo more than a year later, Fort Bowie was the base from which three successive campaigns and a multitude of small supporting expeditions were mounted against the Chiricahuas in Mexico.

Crook began by sending two forces of Regulars and Indian scouts into Mexico, one under Captain Crawford (recalled from Texas), and the other under Lt. Wirt Davis and Lieutenant Gatewood. To prevent the Indians from re-entering the United States, he also stationed cavalry detachments at key water holes along the boundary.

Through the summer and fall of 1885 Crawford and Davis tenaciously pursued the Chiricahuas. Several times the scouts surprised the enemy in their Sierra Madre hiding places, but never did they fight a decisive action. Exhausted, the striking columns reported to Crook at Fort Bowie in October. Preparations were immediately begun for a new campaign.

In November, as Crawford and Davis refitted, a raiding party of 10 warriors slipped into the United States. For a month they rode over 1,900 kilometers through a region patrolled by 83 companies of soldiers, killed 38 whites, captured and wore out 250 horses, and escaped into Mexico with the loss of but one man.

On November 29 Sheridan himself came to Fort Bowie. He suggested to Crook that the solution to the Apache problem lay in removing all the Chiricahuas from Arizona to some distant location, a proposal Crook opposed because of its predictable effect on his scout companies. Probably, too, Sheridan hinted at his increasing lack of confidence in the Indian scouts and his feeling that Regulars offered a surer means to victory, a thesis wholly at variance with Crook's convictions.

While Crook sipped Christmas eggnog at Fort Bowie, Crawford's scouts searched the Sierra Madre for Apaches. Finally, 322 kilometers south of the border, they picked up a trail and, suffering from exhaustion and bitter cold, followed it to a hidden camp. On January 10, 1886, Crawford attacked—only to discover an empty camp. The occupants had fled. But an Apache

Even during the Indian wars, officers and their wives found time for the diversion of a picnic.

Apache scouts pose to have their picture taken.

woman appeared with word that Geronimo and Natchez wanted to come in the next day for a talk. Crawford agreed.

At dawn next morning, before the meeting could be convened, a large force of Mexican militia suddenly attacked Crawford's bivouac. Mounting a rock to signal his identity to his assailants, Crawford was struck in the head by a bullet and killed. As Geronimo and his people watched from surrounding heights, the Apache scouts and Mexican troops exchanged fire for two hours. Then the Mexicans fell back and fortified, and Lt. Marion P. Maus, who had succeeded Crawford in command, persuaded the Mexican officers of their mistake.

Deep in unfriendly country, faced by hostile Apaches and suspicious Mex-

Though one of the oldest members of Geronimo's band, Nana was one of the most steadfast.

No. 176—Council between General Crook and

Natchez

Lt Faison   Capt. Roberts   Cayetano   Tom Blair   Noche   H.W. Daly
      Concepcion   Three Interpr
       Geronimo   Nana   Lieut Maus   José Maria Ya
                            Antonio Bes
                            Jose Montoy

The historic conference in which Geronimo surrendered to Crook took place in the Cañon de los Embudos. Crook, in a sun helmet, is seated at right, flanked by an aide, Capt. John G. Bourke, and young Charley Roberts, son of another aide. Geronimo is seated at left center, facing the camera.

Capt. Bourke   Gen. Crook
                  Charley Roberts

Geronimo's Case

Geronimo was a clever man, a fact well illustrated by this passage. To be sure, he had many grievances against the military and the Indian Bureau, but he does appear to have overstated his case in this speech to General Crook in March 1886:

From here on I want to live at peace. Don't believe any bad talk you hear about me. The agents and the inter- preters hear that somebody has done wrong, and they blame it all on me. Don't believe what they say. I don't want any of this bad talk in the future. I don't want those men who talked this way about me to be my agents any more. I want good men to be my agents and interpreters; people who will talk right. I want this peace to be legal and good. Whenever I meet you I talk good to you, and you to me, and peace is soon established; but when you go to the reservation you put agents and interpreters over us. In the future we don't want these bad men to be allowed near where we are to live. . . . I want to have a good man put over me. While living I want to live well. I know I have to die some time, but even if the heavens were to fall on me, I want to do what is right. I think I am a good man, but in the papers all over the world they say I am a bad man. . . . I never do wrong without a cause. Every day I am think- ing, how am I to talk to you to make you believe what I say; and, I think too, that you are thinking of what you are to say to me. There is one God looking down on us all. We are all children of the one God. God is listen- ing to me. The sun, the darkness, the winds, are all listening to what we now say.

icans, ammunition and food almost gone, Lieutenant Maus decided to return to Fort Bowie. At the end of the first day's march, however, another woman brought word that the Chiricahua leaders still wanted to talk. Two days later, Maus met with Geronimo, Natchez, Nana, and Chihuahua. Geronimo said that he wanted to talk with General Crook about surrender terms and would meet with him near San Bernardino in two moons. As a token of good faith, he yielded nine hostages, including his own and Natchez's wife and Nana. Maus hurried north to report to Crook.

Geronimo would go no farther north than Cañon de los Embudos, 19 kilometers south of the international boundary. Crook and his staff and escort reached this place on March 24, 1886. The Chiricahuas watched suspiciously from a natural fortress atop a lava-covered hill. "A full brigade," noted Crook's aide, "could not drive out that little garrison."

For three days the military and Indian leaders negotiated. Geronimo and Chihuahua recited at great length the wrongs done them by their agents and asserted their own complete innocence of any offense. Crook replied bluntly: "Everything you did on the reservation is known. There is no use for you to try to talk nonsense. I am no child." He demanded unconditional surrender. Otherwise, "I'll keep after you and and kill the last one, if it takes fifty years." But he was bluffing, as Geronimo surely guessed, and finally they reached a compromise. The Apaches would surrender on condition that they and their families be confined somewhere in the East for no longer than two years and then returned to their reservation. On March 27 each of the chiefs made a surrender speech. Crook wrote a dispatch announcing the result and sent it by courier to Fort Bowie for transmission to General Sheridan.

Next morning Crook and his retinue started for Fort Bowie, leaving Lieutenant Maus to escort the prisoners. At their camp, however, Maus discovered that the Indians had obtained mescal from a trader and had drunk themselves into an ugly humor. Throughout the day, as the procession moved slowly northward, they continued to drink. That night, Geronimo and Natchez, with 20 men, 13 women, and 2 children, stole out of camp. Chihuahua, Nana, and a dozen men and 47 women and children remained behind. Maus gave chase as soon as he discovered the defection, but the trail disappeared in the Sierra Madre.

On the very brink of success, Crook's elaborate peace effort had collapsed. Moreover, even before receiving this bad news, Sheridan had informed Crook that the conditional surrender could not be approved. He was to go back to the Indians and demand unconditional surrender. Also, he was to "insure against further hostilities by completing the destruction of the hostiles unless these terms are accepted." In other words, Indians who had surrendered on certain conditions were now to agree to unconditional surrender or be destroyed.

Geronimo's escape aggravated the dispute between the two generals. Sheridan implied that Crook's Indian scouts had aided the escape, or at least had not warned of it, and petulantly directed that a new plan be prepared for protecting settlers against the raids that were sure to come.

Shaken by these developments, on April 1 Crook wired Sheridan a long explanation of his philosophy and methods of Indian relations, and he concluded: "It may be, however, that I am too much wedded to my own views in this matter, and as I have spent nearly eight years of the hardest work of my life in this department, I respectfully request that I may now be relieved from its command." Sheridan complied at once. The next day orders sped to Fort Leavenworth, Kans., for Brig. Gen. Nelson A. Miles to replace Crook as commander of the Department of Arizona.

Ben Wittick

Many of the pictures, especially those of Indians, in this book were taken by George Benjamin Wittick (1845–1903). After service with the Union cavalry, Wittick became interested in photography and set up a studio in Moline, Ill. The lure of the Southwest proved strong, and in 1878 Wittick went to New Mexico as a photographer for the Atlantic and Pacific Railroad. He traveled around Arizona and New Mexico photographing the unfamiliar landscape. Soon, however, he became fascinated with the Apaches, Hopis, Navajos, and Pueblo Indians in the area. The rituals and religious ceremonies, especially the Snake Dance of the Hopis, interested him. In 1903, a rattlesnake that Wittick had caught for some Hopi friends bit him. Three weeks later, Ben Wittick, photographer of the peoples of the Southwest, died.

Brig. Gen. Nelson A. Miles took over the campaign against Geronimo after Crook became disheartened by General Sheridan's loss of confidence and asked to be relieved. Miles had a long career that spanned the years from the Civil War to the early 20th century. He led troops against most of the famous Indian leaders of the time—Crazy Horse, Sitting Bull, Chief Joseph, and Geronimo. In 1894 he commanded troops that stopped the riots connected with the Pullman strike in Chicago. The next year he became Army commander-in-chief and thus figured prominently in the Spanish-American War. He was promoted to lieutenant general in 1901 and retired from active duty two years later. He died in Washington, D. C. in 1925 at the age of 86.

Miles in Command

An able, energetic, and ambitious officer, General Miles plunged into his new assignment with a determination to succeed where Crook, his long-time rival, had failed. First Miles strengthened the network of border outposts that guarded—never effectively—against Apache forays from Mexico. He saw that the high mountains, bright sunlight, and clear atmosphere of the Southwest offered favorable conditions for employing the heliograph. With this device, consisting of mirrors mounted on a tripod, skilled operators could catch the sun's rays and flash messages over distances up to 40 or 50 kilometers away. Miles established 27 heliograph stations covering distinct "districts of observation" and connecting most of the high peaks of southern Arizona and New Mexico. One such station was located on Bowie Mountain, above Fort Bowie. Linked with five other stations, the Bowie Peak installation sent 802 messages and repeated 1,644—more than any other in the system—during the summer of 1886. In each district Miles placed well-equipped columns to intercept any Indians sighted by the observers at the heliograph stations.

Next Miles turned to planning an offensive in Mexico. Sheridan's distrust of the Indian scouts required a new reliance on regular soldiers. To Capt. Henry W. Lawton and an army doctor with command aspirations named Leonard Wood, Miles assigned the task of forming a striking column of specially chosen men. Lawton assembled the command at Fort Huachuca. It consisted of one company of infantry, 35 picked cavalrymen, and 20 Indian scouts. A pack train of 100 mules and 20 packers were to provide daily supply.

Lawton's command left Fort Huachuca on May 5, 1886, and pushed into the Yaqui River country of Sonora. The mountains quickly broke down the cavalry horses and the troopers joined the infantrymen. For four months the column chased the Apaches from one towering mountain range to the next. The 2,250-kilometer trek through the wilds of Mexico demanded uncommon endurance and perseverance. As Leonard Wood recalled the ordeal:

Two of the key leaders of Miles' offensive were Henry Lawton (*left*) and Leonard Wood (*right*). Lawton (1843-1899) later became a major general. Wood (1860-1927) had a spectacular career serving as Army chief of staff (1910-14) and as governor-general of the Philippines (1921-27).

One who does not know this country cannot realize what this kind of service means—marching every day in the intense heat, the rocks and earth being so torrid that the feet are blistered and rifle-barrels and everything metallic being so hot that the hand cannot touch them without getting burnt. It is a country rough beyond description, covered everywhere with cactus and full of rattlesnakes and other undesirable companions of that sort. The rain, when it does come, comes as a tropical tempest, transforming the dry cañons into raging torrents in an instant. . . . We had no tents and little or no baggage of any kind except rations and ammunition. Suits of underclothing formed our uniforms and moccasins covered our feet.

Lawton lost 10 kilograms, Wood, 14. Although the enlisted men had been hand-picked, only one-third of those who had left Fort Huachuca on May 5 remained in the ranks at the end. The rest were replacements for those who had been forced to return to the fort. Three sets of officers had served with the command, only Lawton and Wood staying from beginning to end.

Lawton's campaign, for all its demands on the participants, failed to produce the hoped for results. Only once, on July 14, did the troops come close to cornering the quarry, a Chiricahua camp in a mountain recess 480 kilome-

Troop A, 6th cavalry, stops on the Mexican border during the campaign against Geronimo in 1886.

ters south of the border. The Indian scouts discovered it, but before the Regulars could attack the inhabitants fled. Lawton's relentless pursuit probably wore down and helped discourage the fugitives, but in the end other methods proved more consequential.

Miles had become convinced that success in Mexico depended upon removing the reservation Chiricahuas from Arizona. They provided a commissary, arsenal, and recruit depot for the hostiles and a refuge when the warpath lost its appeal. Persuading officials in Washington to this view, Miles sent troops to the San Carlos Reservation. On August 29, 1886, they assembled the Chiricahuas and marched them to the railroad at Holbrook. Three hundred and eighty-two Indians, including virtually all the scouts who had loyally served Crook, were placed on a train and transported to Fort Marion, Fla.

Earlier, Miles had dispatched a peace mission into Mexico. It consisted of Lt. Charles B. Gatewood and two Chiricahua warriors, Kayitah and Martine. As a scout officer under Crook, Gatewood had become well and favorably known to Geronimo and other Apache leaders. Tracing the hostiles to the vicinity of Fronteras, Sonora, on August 24, 1886, the lieutenant and his companions made camp beside the Bavispe River. Kayitah and Martine went

During the extended pursuits of Geronimo's band, soldiers operated from small temporary camps. The length of time at any one camp varied from one night to about a week. This was a camp of the 4th cavalry in 1885 or 1886.

forward into Geronimo's camp and delivered a demand from General Miles to surrender. Holding Kayitah hostage, Geronimo sent Martine back to say that Gatewood himself must come into the Indian camp.

In a tense confrontation with Geronimo and Natchez, Gatewood repeated Miles' message: "Surrender, and you will be sent with your families to Florida, there to await the decision of the President as to your final disposition. Accept these terms or fight it out to the bitter end." The Indians said they were ready to surrender, but not on those terms. They wanted instead, to go back to San Carlos. "Take us to the reservation—or fight," declared Geronimo. Here Gatewood dropped his surprise revelation. If the hostiles returned to San Carlos, they would find all their kinsmen gone to Florida, and they would have to live alone among other Apache groups long unfriendly to the Chiricahuas. Disconcerted, Geronimo and Natchez asked many questions about General Miles, and then, as the day drew to a close, asked Gatewood what he thought they should do. "Trust General Miles and surrender to him," he replied.

Frederic Remington (1861-1909) spent much time in the west in the company of soldiers, cowboys, prospectors, Indians, and the people of the West and produced more than 3,000 illustrations—black and white drawings and paintings. This painting depicts Lawton's 1886 campaign in the Sierra Madre.

On September 8, 1886, Geronimo and the remainder of the Chiricahuas were assembled on the Fort Bowie parade ground and taken to the waiting trains where they would begin their journey eastward. This picture and the next five chronicle the events of that day. Here the prisoners are assembled on the parade ground just three days after their surrender to General Miles in Skeleton Canyon.

Drawn up in formal dress parade, the garrison turns out as the Chiricahuas depart. Wagons take the Apaches to Bowie Station for the long trip east and an uncertain future.

What thoughts must have been running through the minds of Geronimo (right) and Natchez!

Before the Southern Pacific train pulled out of Bowie Station, the guards posed for a picture. Seated in the center, wearing the high-crowned hat, is Capt. Henry W. Lawton.

Gatewood returned to his own camp. Lawton and Wood had arrived with their men. Anxiously, the troops waited as the Chiricahuas deliberated throughout the night. Next morning, Geronimo and Natchez announced to Gatewood their decision to surrender to General Miles. On the way, however, they must keep their arms, Lawton's command must go along to protect them from other soldiers, and Gatewood must travel with the Apaches and sleep in their camp. To these conditions Gatewood and Lawton agreed. A courier was dispatched to Miles and the procession started north.

Accompanied by an aide and a cavalry escort, General Miles left Fort Bowie on September 2, 1886. The next evening he reached Skeleton Canyon, a defile in the Peloncillo Mountains 95 kilometers southeast of Fort Bowie. Lawton had already arrived, but not without many a tense moment in which the Indians, who still kept a comfortable distance from the soldiers, almost bolted for the mountains as they had after the surrender to Crook.

Geronimo immediately appeared and was introduced to Miles. Regarding the general for a moment, he turned to Gatewood and smiled. "Good, you told the truth," he said. Miles repeated the conditions under which the Indians could surrender. He explained that they would be taken with their families out of Arizona. Thereafter their fate would rest with the President. Geronimo agreed. Next morning he formally surrendered. Natchez, however, remained in the mountains. He was mourning his brother, who had gone back to Mexico in search of stray horses and was thought to have been killed. Accompanied by two interpreters and two scouts, Gatewood went with Geronimo to Natchez' camp and persuaded him to come and talk to Miles. Natchez, too, was pleased with the general and promptly surrendered.

With Geronimo and a troop of cavalry, Miles left Skeleton Canyon on the morning of September 5 and reached Fort Bowie that night. Nearing the post, Geronimo looked at the Chiricahua Mountain and mused: "This is the fourth time I have surrendered." Miles replied: "And I think it is the last time you will ever have occasion to surrender." Three days later Lawton rode in with the rest of the Apaches. Miles had already thrown a cordon of troops around the Bowie military reservation in order to protect Geronimo and Natchez from civil authorities, who wanted to bring them before a Tucson judge and jury. Soldiers speedily disarmed and dismounted the prisoners. On September 8, 1886, they were assembled on the parade ground and, escorted by Lawton's command, left for Bowie Station to be loaded on a train and sent to Florida.

The Apaches also posed for the camera. At right center is Geronimo, and to his right is Natchez.

Recriminations

Elated over the successful outcome of the campaign, President Grover Cleveland telegraphed Miles to hold the prisoners at Fort Bowie until they could be turned over to civil authorities for criminal trial. Miles now had to explain that, like Crook, he had not obtained unconditional surrender. Terms had been granted. Moreover, the prisoners were not at Fort Bowie but already speeding toward Florida. Cleveland promptly ordered them stopped at San Antonio, Texas, until he could learn precisely what terms had been promised. Miles evaded the issue and wrote wordy dispatches that revealed little. After a month of tiresome correspondence, an exasperated President decided that the prisoners could not be honorably released for civil trial and directed that they resume their journey to Florida.

The exile of the Chiricahuas aroused humanitarian groups fighting for Indian rights. They pointed out that Miles' action in taking the friendly Chiricahuas into unhealthful captivity in Florida was bad enough. But to subject men who had served Crook loyally as scouts to the same treatment was worse yet. Even Kayitah and Martine, who had gone with Gatewood to persuade Geronimo to surrender, had been sent to Florida. Also, despite the promise to confine the men with their families, they were placed at Fort Pickens and the women and children at Fort Marion. Finally, removed from their homeland and in a foreign environment, the prisoners began to die in alarming numbers.

The friends of the Indians found powerful allies in Generals Crook and Howard. Crook made speeches, wrote pamphlets, and talked with congressmen and senators in an effort to dramatize the injustice. General Miles and his supporters fought back, and a violent controversy raged that abated only slightly when Crook died in 1890. Nevertheless, largely as a result of the activities of Crook and Howard and the Indian Rights Association, the men at Fort Pickens were united with their families in 1887. A year later they were sent to Mount Vernon Barracks, Alabama, and joined the rest of the

Chiricahuas, who had already been moved to this more healthful location. At last, in 1894, the entire tribe was moved, over the vigorous objections of Miles and the western press, to Fort Sill, Indian Territory (Oklahoma). Here Geronimo died on February 17, 1909. In 1913, 187 Chiricahuas were permitted to transfer to the Mescalero Apache Reservation in New Mexico. The rest chose to remain at Fort Sill, where their descendants live today.

Controversy also rocked the Army over who deserved the credit for Geronimo's surrender. Miles gathered large credit to himself and shared it generously with Lawton and Wood. Friends of Crook indignantly protested the exclusion from the honors of Gatewood, a Crook protégé. In truth, all played important roles—Lawton and Wood by harassing the hostiles, Gatewood by going among them to talk peace, and Miles by skillful management and above all by the removal of the reservation Chiricahuas. But the contrasting fortunes of Miles and his friends, on the one hand, and Gatewood, on the other, left a legacy of lasting bitterness in military circles. Miles rose to top army command. So, later, did Wood. Lawton was a general when killed in the Philippines in 1899. Gatewood, injured in a dynamite explosion, died in 1896, still an obscure first lieutenant.

Last Years of Fort Bowie

The surrender of Geronimo ended the Apache wars and, excepting the Sioux outbreak of 1890, the Indian wars of the West. No longer were the frontier forts to play a significant role in American history. Fort Bowie had outlived its usefulness and its remaining years were placid. The garrison devoted itself to rounding up an occasional Apache who strayed from San Carlos and to investigating reports of Indian depredations. Maneuvers gave the troops field experience, and the mock wars relieved the tedium of garrison life. Finally, on October 17, 1894, Troops B and L, 2d Cavalry, marched out of Fort Bowie and left it to be sold.

Nearby residents obtained construction materials from the buildings of the fort. Erosion set in. And soon it had fallen into ruins. Today these ruins stand as a monument to the American soldier who for more than 20 years endured the hardships and dangers of campaigns that rank among the most arduous in military history. But the ruins also commemorate the Chiricahua Apache Indian. With his blend of fighting qualities and his mastery of guerrilla tactics, he successfully defended his homeland against Spaniards, Mexicans, and Americans for two centuries. In the end he succumbed only when his own kin were mobilized against him.

Today, only the ruins remain of the once bustling Fort Bowie.

*Fort Bowie
National Historic Site, Arizona*

Today visitors may see the ruins of the first and second Fort Bowie. Hike the 2.4-kilometer trail from the parking lot to the ruins. The map is oriented south to help you on your walk.

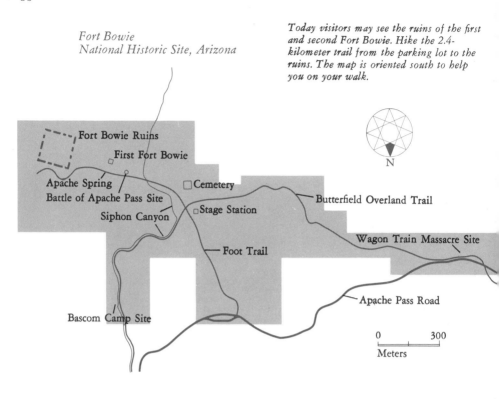

Fort Bowie Ruins

First Fort Bowie

Apache Spring
Battle of Apache Pass Site

Siphon Canyon

Cemetery

Stage Station

Butterfield Overland Trail

Wagon Train Massacre Site

Foot Trail

Apache Pass Road

Bascom Camp Site

N

0   300
Meters

Conversion Tables
(Rounded off to the nearest tenth)

Meters	Feet	Kilograms	Pounds
1	3.3	1	2.2
5	16.4	5	11
10	32.8	10	22
50	164.0	15	33
100	328.1		

Kilometers	Miles
1	0.6
5	3.1
10	6.2
50	31.1
100	62.1
500	310.7
1,000	621.4

Suggested Readings

Adams, Alexander B. *Geronimo: A Biography*. New York, 1971.

Betzinez, Jason, with W. S. Nye. *I Fought with Geronimo*. Harrisburg, Pa., 1959.

Bourke, John G. *An Apache Campaign in the Sierre Madre*. 2d ed., New York, 1958.

_____. *On the Border with Crook*. Chicago, 1891.

Clum, Woodworth. *Apache Agent: The Story of John P. Clum*. New York, 1936.

Crook, George. *General George Crook: His Autobiography*. Edited by Martin F. Schmitt. Norman, Okla., 1946.

Davis, Britton. *The Truth about Geronimo*. New Haven, Conn., 1929.

Dunn, J. P. *Massacres of the Mountains: A History of the Indian Wars of the Far West, 1815–1875*. New York, 1886.

Howard, Oliver O. *My Life and Experiences among Our Hostile Indians*. Hartford, Conn., 1907.

Lockwood, Frank C. *The Apache Indians*. New York, 1936.

Lummis, Charles F. *General Crook and the Apache Wars*. Flagstaff, Ariz., 1966.

Ormsby, Waterman L. *The Butterfield Overland Mail*. Edited by Lyle H. Wright and Josephine M. Bynum. San Marino, Calif., 1955.

Thrapp, Dan L. *Al Sieber, Chief of Scouts*. Norman, Okla., 1964.

_____. *The Conquest of Apacheria*. Norman, Okla., 1967.

_____. *General Crook and the Sierra Madre Adventure*. Norman, Okla., 1972.

Utley, Robert M. *Frontier Regulars: The United States Army and the Indian, 1866–1891*. New York, 1973.

_____. *Frontiersmen in Blue: The United States Army and the Indian, 1848–1865*. New York, 1967.

Photo Credits.
Arizona Historical Society: 8, 13, 22, 24,
29, 30–31, 35, 36, 42, 49, 50 (left and
right), 51 (bottom), 52 (top and bottom),
54, 57, 58 (bottom), 59 (top and bottom),
63, 70 (right), 71, 72, 74–75, and 76–77.
Gatewood Collection, Arizona Historical
Society: 53, 64–65, and 78.
French Collection, Arizona Pioneer
Historical Society, Tucson: 58 (top).
Museum of New Mexico: 19, 27, 39, 45,
and 67.
Bill Jones: 12–13, 14, 84–85.
Library of Congress: 16 and 28.
U.S. Army Signal Corps/National Archives:
32, 46–47, 51 (top), 62, 70 (left), 73,
and 80.
Oregon Historical Society: 34.
Bowen Collection/Custer Battlefield
National Monument: 68.

NPS 175

Library of Congress Cataloging in Publication Data
Utley, Robert Marshall, 1929-
   A clash of cultures.
      1. Apache Indians—Wars. 2. Fort Bowie, Ariz.—
History. I. Title.
E99.A6U89   979.1'53'04   75-619282

☆ U.S. GOVERNMENT PRINTING OFFICE : 1984 O - 457-415

For sale by the U.S. Government Printing Office
Superintendent of Documents, Mail Stop: SSOP, Washington, DC 20402-9328